The Story of a Special Day
Volume 221

August

8

The 220th day of the year (221st in leap years).
There are 145 days remaining until the end of the year.

by Michael Dobson

Timespinner
Press

This book is also available in e-book form for Kindle, e-pub devices, and other formats from your favorite online booksellers.

For more information about the series, about us, or about your special day, please email us at editor@timespinnerpress.com.

Look for other volumes in *The Story of a Special Day,* coming often. See www.timespinnerpress.com for details and for the most recent information.

Table of Contents

For the definition of "O.S.," "CE," and "BCE" used with some dates , see the section "On Names and Dates."

Cover: "Defeat of the Spanish Armada 8 August 1588," by Philip James de Loutherbourgh (Courtesy National Maritime Museum, London).

Quote of the Day

"When you speak of a train robbery, this involves no actual loss of train, but rather the contents of the train, which were pilfered."

Peter Cook and Allen Bennett, in the comedy revue *Beyond the Fringe*. The Great Train Robbery took place in England on August 8, 1963 .

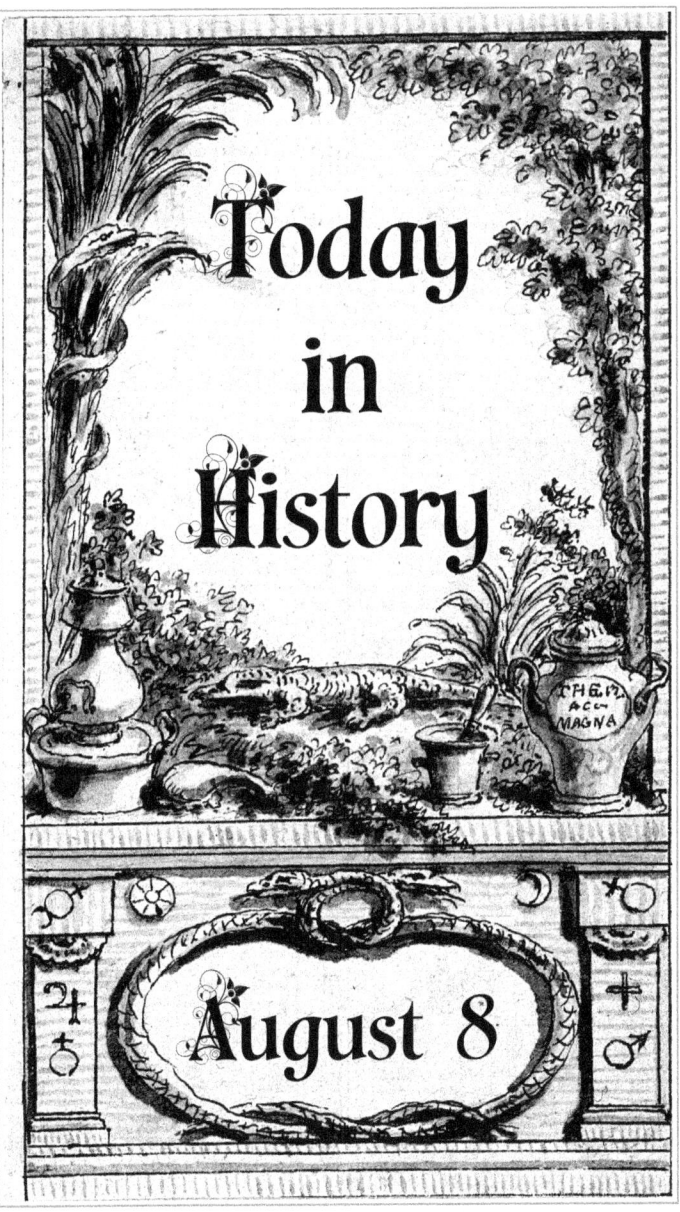

Today in History

August 8

The Spanish Armada Leaving the Port of Ferrol
by Sir Oswald W. Brierly

Event of the Day
Spanish Armada Defeated

The *Grande y Felicísima Armada* ("Great and Most Fortunate Navy"). known in English history as the Spanish Armada, was finally defeated at the Battle of Gravelines on August 8, 1588.

The Armada Departs

The armada, consisting of 151 ships manned by 8,000 sailors and 18,000 soldiers, set sail on May 28, 1588, for England. Its mission was to overthrow Elizabeth I of England and restore Catholic rule in that nation, as well as to stop English meddling in the Dutch Revolt against Spain.

Philip II, ruler of Spain and Portugal, had also been King of England during his marriage to Elizabeth's predecessor, Mary I, called "Bloody Mary" for her persecution of Protestants. He had already sponsored several plots to have Elizabeth overthrown and replaced by her cousin Mary Queen of Scots, but Elizabeth had her executed in 1587.

With the support of Pope Sixtus V, Philip II levied "crusade taxes" to build his fleet, and appointed an experienced commander, Álvaro de Bazán, to take charge of the invasion. Unfortunately, Bazán died before the fleet could be launched. His replacement, the Duke of Medina Sidonia was a courtier with no experience at sea.

The Spanish Armada took two full days for all ships to leave port. Their destination was the coast of Flanders, then part of the greater Netherlands, where 30,000 more soldiers under the command of the Duke of Parma were waiting to be carried across the Channel to invade England.

The Voyage of the Armada

Bad weather hampered the Armada as it sailed up the coast. The English first sighted the Spanish fleet on July 19, but trapped by tide, were late getting to sea. By the night of July 20, the English fleet was able to tack upwind of the Armada, gaining the weather gage.

At the break of day on July 21, the two fleets clashed off the coast of Plymouth, England, near the Eddystone Rocks. The English fleet, commanded by Lord Howard of Effingham, with Sir Francis Drake as Vice Admiral, was larger than that of the Spanish but greatly inferior in firepower.

The first day's engagement was not decisive. The English fleet had superior speed and maneuverability, but their long range cannon fire was ineffective. That night, Sir Francis Drake managed to loot some of the damaged Spanish ships for gunpowder and gold, but in the darkness his fleet was scattered. It took a full day for the English to regroup, by which time the Armada had sailed closer to its destination.

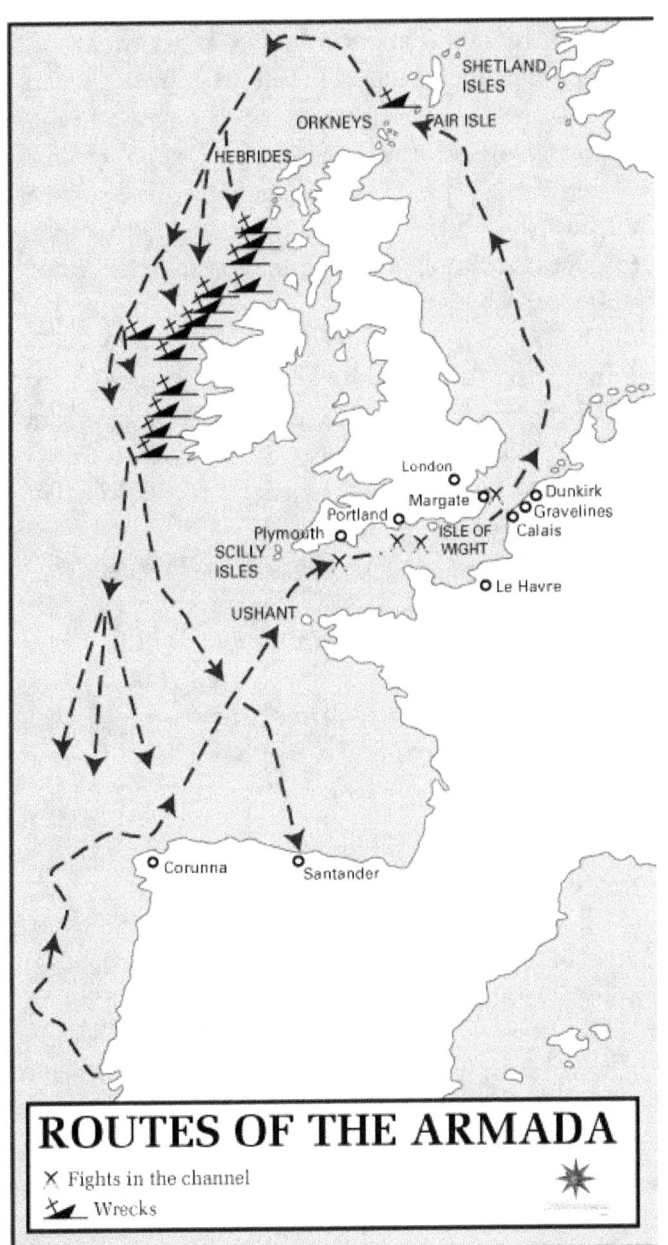

ROUTES OF THE ARMADA

X Fights in the channel

X⤳ Wrecks

On July 23 the fleets engaged in another indecisive engagement. Unable to gain shelter in only secure harbor within reach, the Armada made sail for Calais without waiting for Parma's army.

By July 27, the Armada reached Calais. Disease had whittled Parma's army from 30,000 to a mere 16,000, and worse, it would take at least six days for the transport-poor army to arrive.

The English, however, would not wait. At midnight on July 28, they sent eight fireships — warships filled with pitch and brimstone and set alight — downwind into the Spanish fleet. The Spanish scattered in disorganized confusion. The English closed in.

After the two earlier battles, the English had learned that they needed to close within 100 yards for their cannons to penetrate the oak hulls of the Spanish warships, but they were short of gunpowder. At the same time, they feared getting too close, because the Spanish would ensnare their ships with grappling hooks and board.

The Battle of Gravelines

The culmination came on August 8, 1588, at the Battle of Gravelines off the border of Flanders. The superior maneuverability of the English ships proved decisive. Again and again the English closed, firing cannon broadsides into the enemy ships. The battle raged for eight hours until the English, low on ammunition, were forced to disengage. Toward the end of the battle, some gunners were loading chains into their cannon.

The Spanish lost five ships. Worse, they were no longer in a position to rendezvous with the Duke of Parma. But they were still a formidable and dangerous foe, and the danger to the English was far from over.

The Armada withdrew to the north, pursued by the English even though they were nearly out of ammunition. By the time the two fleets neared the coast of Scotland, the English broke off the pursuit. Unable to complete his mission, the Duke of Medina Sedonia could only chart his course for home by the more hazardous route of traveling around Scotland and Ireland in the treacherous waters or the North Atlantic.

The ships were first pulled off course by the Gulf Stream current. Unable to measure longitude, the Armada turned south much farther to the west than they had planned. Ice and storms took more ships than had been lost to the English. Some 5,000 men perished; others were shipwrecked on the coast of Ireland, never to return home.

Destruction of the Invincible Armada, by José Gartner de la Peña

The Wright Model A airplane at Le Mans

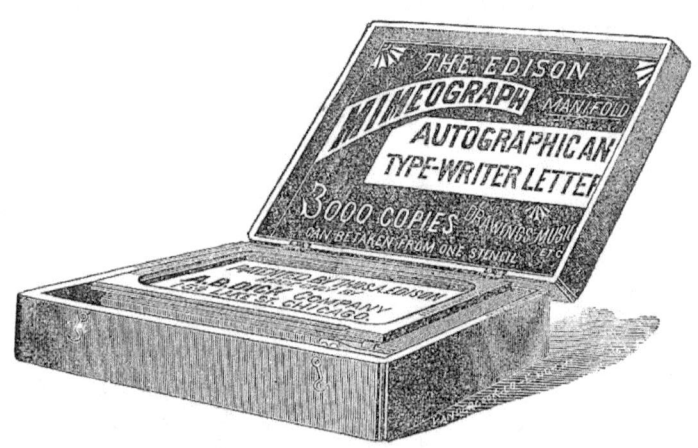

An advertisement for the Edison Mimeograph

What Happened on August 8?

From the creation of great works of engineering and art, to devastating wars and natural disasters, thousands of years of history have left their mark on each and every day of the year. Here are some important events that occurred on August 8. (Items with a photo or illustration are boxed.)

1786 — Jaques Balmat and Michel Paccard successfully scale **the highest mountain in the Alps,** Switzerland's Mont Blanc, an exploit considered the **beginning of modern mountaineeering.**

1863 — Following his **defeat at the Battle of Gettysburg, General Robert E. Lee sends a letter of resignation** to Confederate President Jefferson Davis, who refuses it.

1876 — Inventor **Thomas Edison receives a patent** for a system of "autographic printing," later licensed by A. B. Dick under the trademark **"mimeograph."**

1908 — Inventor Wilbur Wright makes the **first public airplane flight,** lasting one minute 45 seconds, near Le Mans, France.

1918 — **World War I: The Battle of Amiens begins** the "Hundred Days Offensive that would ultimately lead to the end of the war.

1942 — Mahatma Gandhi launches the "Quit India" Movement (भारत छोड़ो hआन्दोलन *Bhārat Chhodho Āndolan*), **demanding an end to British rule of India.** Gandhi and other independence leaders are immediately arrested.

1945 — The London Charter, **establishing the laws and procedures for the Nuremberg trials** following the defeat of Nazi Germany in World War II, is issued.

1946 — First flight of the Convair B-36 Peacemaker, the largest mass-produced piston-engined aircraft ever built; it would be the primary nuclear weapons delivery vehicle of the United States until 1955.

First flight of the B-36

1963 — In what became known as **The Great Train Robbery,** a gang of 15 robbers attacked a Royal Mail train between Glasgow and London, stealing over £2.6 million (equivalent to £49.1 million today), most of which was never recovered. *(Also see page 17)*

1969 — Photographer Iain Macmillan takes the iconic photograph that will become **the cover to The Beatles'** *Abbey Road.*

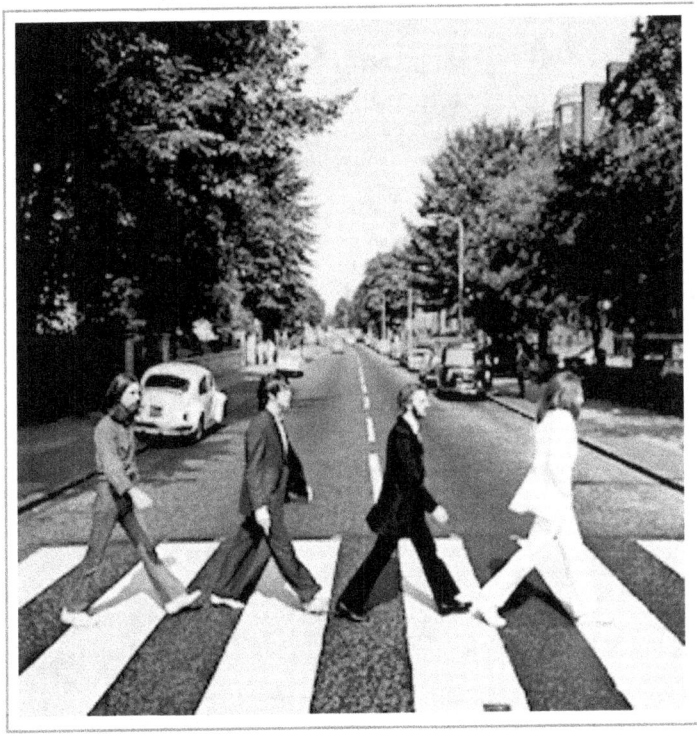

Cover photograph from The Beatles' *Abbey Road*

1973 — South Korean dissident leader **Kim Dae-jung** (김대중) **is kidnapped** by agents of the ruling government and held for five days. Kim Dae-jung would later become President of South Korea and receive the 2000 Nobel Peace Prize.

1974 — Faced with the prospect of impeachment and removal from office, US President **Richard Nixon announces his resignation** in a nationally-televised speech. His resignation would take effect at noon the following day.

1991 — The **Warsaw Radio Mast**, which became the world's tallest structure in 1974, **collapses.** It remains the second tallest structure ever built, second only to 2010's Burj Kalifa.

2000 — The **pioneering Confederate submarine** *H.L. Hunley*, sunk for the third time on February 17, 1864, **is raised** from the sea floor.

Submarine Torpedo Boat H. L. Hunley, by Conrad Wise Chapman

Quote of the Day

"I'd rather die on my feet, than live on my knees."

Emiliano Zapata, revolutionary leader
born August 8, 1879

Births
and
Deaths

THERI
ACA
MAGNA

August 8

Fay Wray, starred in *King Kong* (1934), died August 8, 2004

Notable August 8 People

With the current world population at about seven billion people, on average about 19 million people also celebrate their birthdays on August 8 — and that isn't counting millions and millions who came before! No matter when you were born, you share your birthday with many special people whose accomplishments (and occasionally embarrassments) have been noted as part of history.

In this section, you'll meet fascinating people who share your birthday. They're organized by what they're famous for, and then in reverse chronological order from most recent to earliest. Those who are shown in photographs or artwork have a box around them. We don't have photos of everyone, so please forgive us if your favorite person is missing.

Some of these people you've heard of, others will be new to you, but they all make up an important part of the reason that August 8 is a truly special day!

Matthew Henson

Who Was Born on August 8?

Crime and Punishment

Ronnie Biggs, criminal known for his role in The Great Train Robbery *(see pg, 9)*, which took place on his 34th birthday. He lived as a fugitive for 36 years before being sentenced to prison in 2001. *(1929)*

Exploration and Adventure

Svetlana Yevgenyevna Savitskaya, Soviet cosmonaut, first woman to fly into space twice, first woman to perform a spacewalk. *(1948)*

Dennis Tito, American engineer and entrepreneur who became the first "space tourist"in2001 by self-funding a trip to the International Space Station. *(1940)*

Matthew Henson, first African-American Arctic explorer; accompanied Admiral Robert Peary on seven attempts to reach the North Pole. *(1866)*

Fashion

Rudy Gernreich, fashion designer known for the topless "monokini" bathing suit and for his unisex costumes for the television series *Space: 1999. (1922)*

Government and Military

Mohammed Morsi (محمد مرسي), first democratically elected president of Egypt; deposed by the military following his attempt to grant himself unlimited power to legislate. *(1951)*

Arthur Goldberg, US Supreme Court justice and Ambassador to the United Nations. *(1908)*

Emiliano Zapata, leading figure in the Mexican Revolution, considered a national hero of Mexico. *(1879)*

Esther Hobart Morris, first woman justice of the peace in the United States. *(1814)*

Cecil Calvert, 2nd Baron Baltimore, first proprietor and governor of the Province of Maryland and governor of the Colony of Newfoundland. *(1605)*

Invention

Ken Kutaragi (久夛良木 健), Sony Computer Entertainment CEO and engineer known as the "Father of the PlayStation" for his leadership and technical role in developing the gaming console. *(1950)*

Emiliano Zapata (Courtesy George Grantham Bain Collection)

Journalism and Letters

Deborah Norville, television journalist best known as co-host of *The Today Show* and as anchor of *Inside Edition. (1958)*

Jostein Gaarder, author of the international best-seller *Sophie's World: A Novel About the History of Philosophy. (1952)*

Randy Shilts, pioneering gay journalist, author of the 1987 best-selling book *And the Band Played On: Politics, People, and the AIDS Epidemic. (1951)*

Marjorie Kinnan Rawlings, won the 1939 Pulitzer Prize for fiction for her novel *The Yearling. (1896)*

Sara Teasdale, American lyric poet. *(1884)*

Medicine

George Tiller, physician assassinated while serving as an usher in his church by an anti-abortion extremist for his work as medical director of the Wichita (Kansas) Women's Health Care Services clinic. *(1941)*

Bob Smith, physician who co-founded Alcoholics Anonymous. *(1866)*

Sara Teasdale (Photo: Arnold Genthe)

Music and Dance

JC Chasez, singer-songwriter and producer known as a member of the boy band *NSYNC. (1976)

The Edge (David Evans), lead guitarist of the rock band U2. *(1961)*

Anton Fig, drummer best known for his work with the CBS Orchestra on *Late Night With David Letterman. (1952)*

Joe Tex, African-American singer known for his hits "Hold What You've Got," "Skinny Legs and All," "I Gotcha," and "Ain't Gonna Bump No More (With No Big Fat Woman." *(1935)*

Serena Wilson dancer and choreographer who help popularize and legitimize belly dancing in the United States. *(1933)*

Mel Tillis, country music singer-songwriter whose hits include "I Ain't Never," "Good Woman Blues," and "Coca-Cola Cowboy," winner of the National Medal of Arts. *(1932)*

Webb Pierce, honky tonk musician known for "In the Jailhouse Now," "I Don't Care," and "There Stands the Glass;" member of the Country Music Hall of Fame. *(1921)*

Jimmy Witherspoon, American jump blues singer best remembered for his hit "Ain't Nobody's Business If I Do." *(1920)*

Benny Carter, jazz multi-instrumentalist and bandleader; received the NEA Jazz Masters Award, a Grammy Lifetime Achievement Award, and the National Medal of the Arts. *(1907)*

Benny Carter at the Apollo Theater, 1946. (Photo: William Gottlieb)

Performing Arts

Lee Unkrich, animation director who won the Academy Award for Best Animated Film for *Toy Story 3*. *(1967)*

Robin Quivers, radio personality best known as the co-host of *The Howard Stern Show*. *(1952)*

Martin Brest, producer and screenwriter known for *Beverly Hills Cop, Midnight Run, Scent of a Woman,* and other films. *(1951)*

Keith Carradine, member of the Carradine acting family; known for roles in such series as *Deadwood, Dexter,* and *Madam Secretary,* as well as for numerous films. He won an Academy Award for Best Original Song for "I'm Easy," for the film *Nashville,* in which he played Tom Frank. *(1949)*

Connie Stevens, actress known for the television series *Hawaiian Eye* and numerous film roles; recorded the hit novelty song, "Kookie, Kookie, Lend Me Your Comb," based on her appearances on the TV series *77 Sunset Strip*. *(1938)*

Dustin Hoffman, actor best known for *The Graduate* (1967), *Kramer vs. Kramer* (1980), and *Rain Man* (1989), among many others; won the Academy Award for Best Actor for the latter two films. *(1937)*

Donald P. Bellisario, television producer known for *Magnum , P.I., Airwolf, Quantum Leap, JAG, NCIS,* and others. *(1935)*

Dustin Hoffman (1968)

Esther Williams

Terry Nation, television writer known for his contributions to *Doctor Who* (including the creation of the Daleks); created the series *Blake's 7. (1930)*

Richard Anderson, actor who appeared in such films as *Forbidden Planet, Zorro, The Long, Hot Summer,* and *Seven Days in May;* best remembered as Oscar Goldman from the television series *The Six Million Dollar Man* and *The Bionic Woman. (1926)*

Rory Calhoun, actor known for his roles in such films as *Spellbound, How to Marry a Millionaire, River of No Return,* and the television series *The Texan. (1922)*

Esther Williams, champion competitive swimmer and actress, famous for her "aquamusicals," including the 1952 hit *Million Dollar Mermaid. (1921)*

William Asher, television director and producer involved with such series as *Our Miss Brooks, I Love Lucy,* and *Bewitched. (1921)*

Dino De Laurentiis, produced over 500 films, including 38 Academy Award nominees. *(1919)*

Rosetta LeNoire, stage and screen actress and producer best remembered for her role as "Mother" Winslow on the television series *Family Matters.* Awarded the National Medal of the Arts. *(1911)*

Science and Medicine

Paul Dirac, shared the 1933 Nobel Prize in Physics for his work in atomic theory. *(1902)*

Ernest O. Lawrence, won the 1939 Nobel Prize in Physics for his invention of the cyclotron; founded the Lawrence Livermore National Laboratory. *(1901)*

Sports

Rinku Singh, Indian baseball pitcher for the Pittsburgh Pirates organization, subject of the 2014 Disney film *Million Dollar Arm.* (1988)

Anita Włodarczyk, won two Olympic gold medals in the hammer throw, first woman in history to throw the hammer over 80 meters. *(1985)*

Roger Federer, Olympic gold medalist and professional tennis player, winner of numerous titles. *(1981)*

Craig Breslow, MLB pitcher called "the smartest man in baseball" for his undergraduate major at Yale in molecular biophysics and biochemistry. *(1980)*

Marcello Balboa, played football (soccer) for the US national team; member of the National Soccer Hall of Fame. *(1967)*

Chris Eubank, boxer, held the WBO middleweight and super-middleweight boxing titles. *(1966)*

Ernest O. Lawrence (right, with M. Stanley Livingston) in front of the 27-inch cyclotron at the University of California Berkeley (1934)

Bruce Matthews, NFL offensive lineman for the Houston Oilers and Tennessee Titans, member of the Pro Football Hall of Fame. *(1961)*

Herbert Prohaska, Austrian football (soccer) player named as their most outstanding player of the past fifty years. *(1955)*

Ken Dryden, member of the Hockey Hall of Fame, served in the Canadian Parliament and as a cabinet minister. *(1947)*

Frank Howard, baseball outfielder, coach, and manager for the Los Angeles Dodgers, Washington Senators, and Texas Rangers; named 1960's NL Rookie of the Year. *(1936)*

Jerry Tarkanian, basketball coach and player known for his long tenure with the UNLV Runnin' Rebels; member of the Naismith Memorial Basketball Hall of Fame. *(1930)*

James "Jumbo" Elliott, track and field coach who produced five Olympic gold medal winners, member of the Track and Field Hall of Fame. *(1915)*

Jerry Tarkanian surrounded by members of his basketball team

Self portrait of James Tissot, circa 1865

Who Died on August 8?

Art

James Tissot, French painter and illustrator. *(1902)*

Eugène Boudin, French landscape painter. *(1898)*

Business

John H. Johnson, founded the Johnson Publishing Company, first African-American to appear on the Forbes 400 list of the richest Americans. *(2005)*

Fergus McMaster, aviation pioneer who co-founded the Queensland and Northern Territory Aerial Services Limited, more commonly known as Qantas. *(1950)*

Journalism and Letters

Ellen Raskin, children's novelist best known for the 1979 Newberry winning *The Westing Game. (1984)*

Nicholas Monsarrat, novelist known for his novels *The Cruel Sea, The Tribe That Lost Its Head,* and others. *(1979)*

Vilhelm Moberg, Swedish journalist and author known for his series *The Emigrants,* made into an Academy Award-nominated film of the same name. *(1973)*

Shirley Jackson, author best known for her 1948 short story "The Lottery" and her 1959 novel *The Haunting of Hill House. (1965)*

Military and Adventure

James Irvin, American astronaut who served as Lunar Module pilot for the Apollo 15 mission. *(1991)*

Madeleine de Verchères, Canadian heroine famed for thwarting an Iroquois raid on her community at the age of fourteen. *(1747)*

Music

Cannonball Adderley, jazz saxophonist during the "hard bob" era, member of the *Down Beat* Jazz Hall of Fame. *(1975)*

Johnny Dodds, jazz clarinetist and saxophonist, member of the *Down Beat* Jazz Hall of Fame. *(1940)*

Performing Arts

Karen Black, actress known for *Easy Rider, Five Easy Pieces, The Great Gatsby,* and many others. *(2013)*

Patricia Neal, actress known for such films as *The Day the Earth Stood Still, Breakfast at Tiffany's,* and *Hud,* for which she won an Academy Award for Best Actress. *(2010)*

Patricia Neal

Barbara Bel Geddes, stage, film, and television actress best known for playing Miss Ellie on the television series *Dallas. (2005)*

Fay Wray, actress best known for playing the female lead in the 1933 film *King Kong. (2004)* *(Photo pg. 14)*

Alan Napier, theatrical, film, and television actor best remembered for playing the butler Alfred in the 1960s live action *Batman* television series. (1988)

Louise Brooks, actress who began in the silent film era and went on to make talkies, remembered as the iconic image of a flapper and for popularizing the bobbed haircut. *(1985)*

Louise Brooks (Courtesy George Grantham Bain)

Richard Deacon, actor best known as Mel Cooley on *The Dick Van Dyke Show* and as Fred Rutherford on *Leave It To Beaver. (1984)*

Cast of *The Dick Van Dyke Show* (1962)
(L-R) Morey Amsterdam, **Richard Deacon**, Mary Tyler Moore, Dick Van Dyke, Rose Marie

Record-Setters

Angus MacAskill, 7 ft. 9 in. man cited by the
Guinness Book of World Records as the tallest non-
pathological giant in recorded history. *(1863)*

Religion

Mary MacKillop, first Australian saint, known for
founding the Sisters of St. Joseph of the Sacred
Heart. *(1909)*

Science

Sir Nevill Francis Mott, won the 1977 Nobel Prize in
Physics for his work on the electronic structure of
magnetic and disordered systems. *(1996)*

Sports

Wilbert Robinson, baseball catcher, coach, and
manager elected in 1945 to the Baseball Hall of Fame.
(1934)

Launceston Elliot, Scottish weightlifter and first
British Olympic champion. *(1930)*

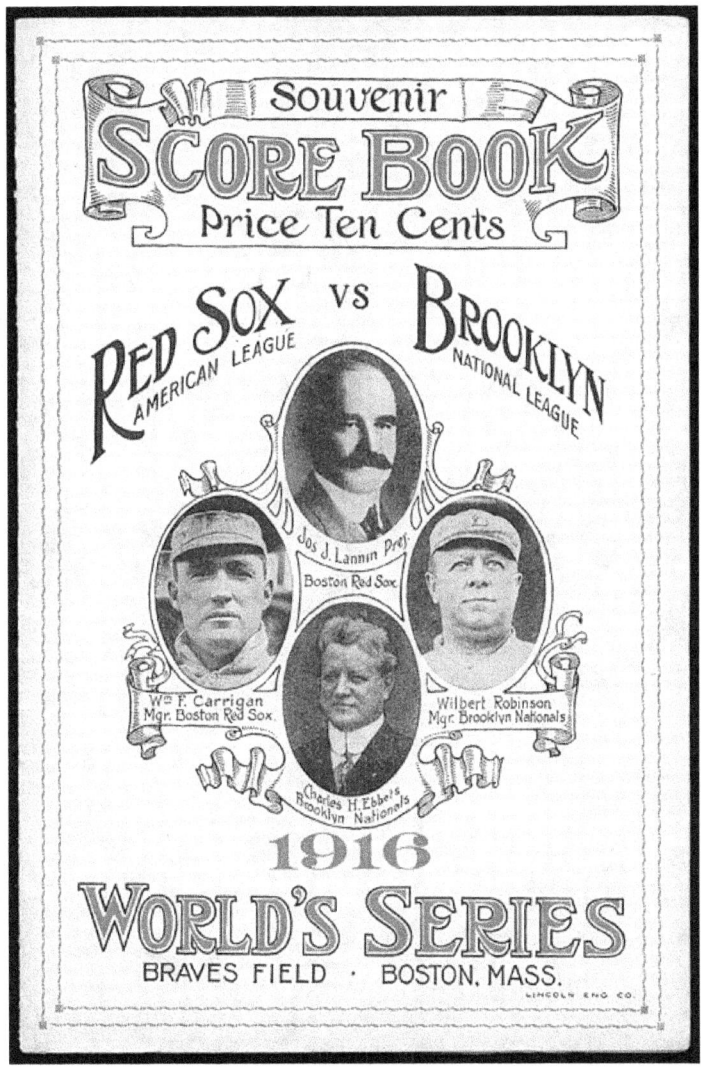

Souvenir program from the 1916 World Series. Wilbert Robinson is on the right.

Quote of the Day

"I have never been a quitter."

Richard Nixon, US President
in his resignation address, August 8, 1974

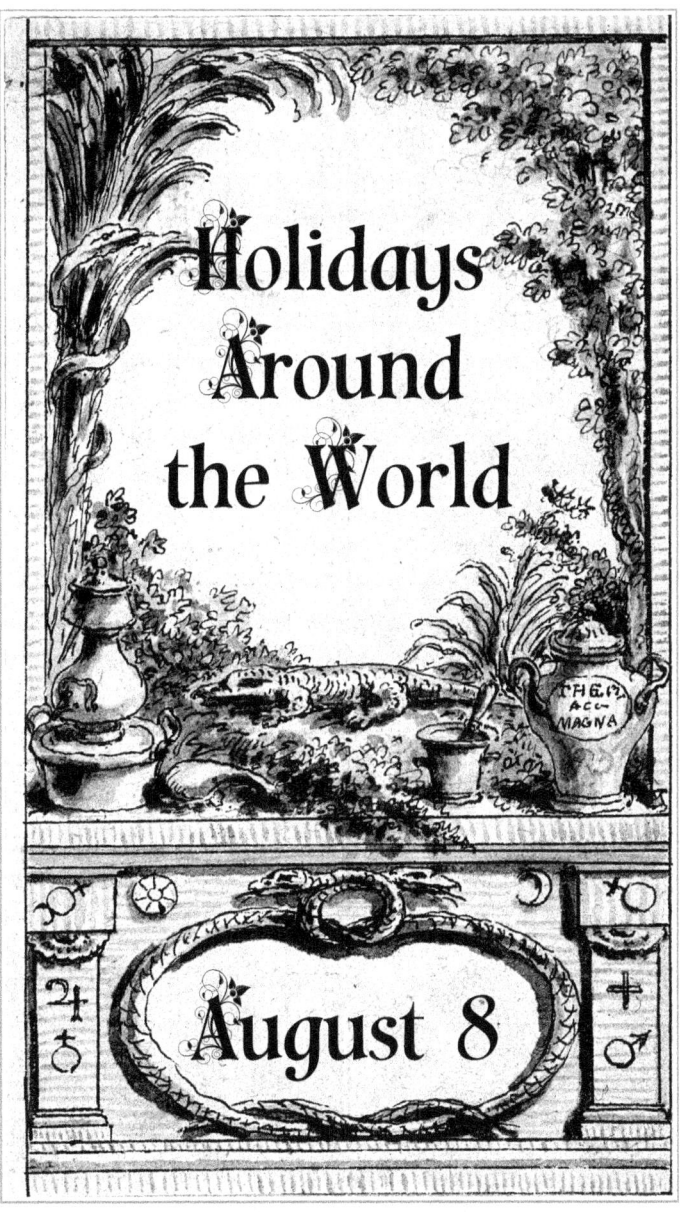

Holidays
Around
the World

CHEM
ACU
MAGNA

August 8

For International Cat Day: "Young Ballerina Holding a Black Cat,"
Pierre Carrier-Belleuse (1895)

Holidays Around the World

If you're looking for a reason to take your special day off, you should know that every single day is a holiday somewhere in the world! Here's some of what you can celebrate on August 8!

General Events

Ceasefire Day (Iraq and Iraqi Kurdistan)
Celebrates the end of the Iran-Iraq War. *(Always August 8)*

Bā bā Day (爸爸節) (Mongolia, Taiwan)
Father's Day in Mongolia and Taiwan is celebrated on the eighth day of the eighth month, because *bā bā* (literally 8-8) means dad (爸爸 or "bàba"). *(Always August 8)*

International Cat Day (worldwide)
Created by the International Fund for Animal Welfare, International Cat Day is celebrated each August 8. (National Cat Day in the US is celebrated on October 29; World Cat Day is celebrated on February 17 in Europe and on March 1 in Russia.) *(Always August 8)*

Namnsdag (Sweden)
The Namesday of the Queen is an official flag day in Sweden. *(Always August 8)*

Nane Nane Day (Tanzania)

"Nane nane" literally means "eight-eight" in Swahili. In Tanzania, the day recognizes the important contribution of farmers to the Tanzanian economy. (*Always August 8*)

Food Holidays

In the United States, almost every day of the year is dedicated to a particular food. (Some other countries do this also, but not every day.) Sponsored by manufacturers, retailers, farmers, or simply fans, these days are often proclaimed by the President, Congress, state governors, or mayors. Given that there are more different foods than days of the year, some days honor more than one kind of food!

August 8 is **National Frozen Custard Day** and also **National Zucchini Day.** You probably want to finish your zucchini before you start on your frozen custard.

In addition, the entire month of August is used to celebrate numerous foods. Here's a list of what to eat in the month of August!

- National Catfish Month
- National Panini Month
- National Peach Month
- National Sandwich Month

Sign advertising frozen custard (Photo: Jose Kevo, CC BY-SA 2.0)

Christian Feast Days and Holidays

Each day in the year is considered a feast day for one or more saints. They are somewhat different in western Christianity (Catholicism and many forms of Protestantism) and in eastern (Orthodox) Christianity. There are many others; this is a selection.

In *Western Christianity*, it is the feast day of Saints Cyriacus, Dominic de Guzmán, Hormisdas, Largus, Mary MacKillop, and Smaragdus.

In *Eastern Orthodox Christianity*, it is also the commemoration of Saints Myron the Wonderworker, Emilian the Confessor, Severus, Mummolus, Gedeon, Zosimas the Sinaite, and Philaret of Ichalka. (These are observed on July 26 by "Old Calendarists.")

Honorary Months

Presidents, Congresses, and nations around the world issue proclamations recognizing particular months to honor certain causes. These events generally fall in August, though honorary months do come and go. Holidays established by states and nonprofit organizations are listed if verified. If not otherwise specified, all months are US. There is some variation from year to year; some celebratory months get added and others get dropped. Two places to get up to date information are the current edition of *Chase's Calendar of Events* or the website Brownielocks (www.brownielocks.com). Here are some honorary designations for August.

- American Adventures Month
- American Artists Appreciation Month
- American Indian Heritage Month
- Audio Appreciation Month
- Bystander Awareness Month
- Children's Eye Health and Safety Month
- Child Support Awareness Month
- National Children's Vision and Learning Month
- Digestive Tract Paralysis (DTP) Month

- Get Ready for Kindergarten Month *(Photo next page)*

- Month of Philippine Languages (Philippines)
- National Back to School Month
- National Black Business Month
- National Breastfeeding Month
- National Goat Cheese Month
- National Immunization Awareness Month
- National Lawn Games Month
- National Minority Donor Awareness Month
- National Water Quality Month
- Neurosurgery Outreach Month
- Psoriasis Awareness Month
- Spinal Muscular Atrophy Awareness Month
- What Will Be Your Legacy Month
- Win with Civility Month
- Family Meals Month
- Tomboy Tools Month
- Win With Civility Month

GET READY FOR KINDERGARTEN MONTH. A photograph from a nursery school operated for women working in the war effort, 1943. (Photo: Marjory Collins for the Farm Security Administration, Office of War Information)

Moveable and Multi-Day Events

Some events take place over a specific week or time period. Start and finish dates may vary from year to year. Some events occur on different days each year (such as "fourth Saturday of a month"). These events sometimes take place on August 8.

Sunday on or closest to August 9 (August 7-12)
- National Peacekeepers' Day (Canada)

2nd Sunday (August 8-14)
- Children's Day (Argentina, Chile, Uruguay)
- Father's Day (Brazil. Samoa)
- Melon Day (Turkmenistan)
- Navy Day (Bulgaria)

2nd Monday (August 8-14)
- Heroes' Day (Zimbabwe)
- Father's Day (Samoa) (Monday after the second Sunday in August)
- Victory Day (Hawaii and Rhode Island)

2nd Tuesday (August 8-14)
- Defence Forces Day (Zimbabwe)

2nd Saturday (August 8-14)
- Sports Day (Russia)

Just for Fun

Anybody can make up a holiday, and many people do! While none of these are officially recognized and some may come and go, here are a few more holidays for August 8.

- Dalek Day (celebrating the birth of Dalek creator Terry Nation)
- Happiness Happens Day (Secret Society of Happy People)
- Sneak Some Zucchini Onto Your Neighbor's Porch Night (follows National Zucchini Day)

About
the
Month
of

August

"August," from the *Brevarium Grimani* by Simon Bening (c.1510)

August: The Eighth Month

In the parching August wind,
Cornfields bow the head,
Sheltered in round valley depths,
On low hills outspread.
        — "A Year's Windfalls," Christina G. Rossetti

In ancient Rome, the month we know as August was originally known as *Sextilis*, meaning sixth. That's because the Roman calendar of the time had March as the first month of the year. It originally had only 29 days, but in his great calendar reform in 45 BCE, Julius Caesar added two days to the month. In 8 BCE, the month was renamed August in honor of Augustus, first emperor of Rome.

It's often claimed that Augustus stole one of February's days to add to his month, but the month already had 31 days long before Augustus became emperor. Augustus chose the month because it was the time of year in which he had accomplished some of his greatest triumphs, including the conquest of Egypt.

In both the Julian and Gregorian calendars, August is the eighth month of the year. It's one of seven months that have 31 days. During leap years, August and February start on the same day of the week; in non-leap years years, no month begins on the same day of the week as August. However, August and November always end on the same day of the week, regardless of the type of year.

In the Northern Hemisphere, August is a summer month, and in many European countries, the holiday month for most workers. In the Southern Hemisphere, August is the equivalent to February, deep in winter. No matter which hemisphere, August is a good month to spot a meteor; the Perseid Meteor Shower always takes place during the month.

August is also the month in the US that has the highest birthrate.

August in Other Cultures

The month of August has different names in different languages. Some nations use calendars other than the Gregorian, and their months may overlap with June. In lunar-based calendars, such as Islam, months move through the seasons. Still, many languages often have a word for August itself.

Albanian: Gusht

Arabic (Egypt, Sudan, Yemen): يونأغسطس (Aġustus)

Arabic (Levant): حزيراآب ('āb)

Arabic (Libya): الصهانيبال (hānībāl)

Arabic (Algeria and Tunisia): جوأوت (Ūt)

Arabic (Morocco): غشت (ġušt)

Azerbaijani: Avqust

Basque: Abuztu

Chinese: 八月 (Cantonese: baatyuht; Mandarin: bāyuè; Taiwanese: peh-goeh)

Croatian: Kolovoz

Czech: Srpen

Finnish: Elokuu

French: Août

German (Swiss): Auguscht (in other German dialects, it's just "August.")

Greek: Αύγουστος (Aúgoustos)

Hebrew: יואוגוסט (âvgûst)

Hindi: अगस्त (agast)

Hungarian: Augusztus

Irish (Gaelic): Lúnasa mí Lúnasa

Italian: Agosto

Japanese (traditional calendar): 九月 (kugatsu), 長月 (nagatsuki)

Korean: 팔월 (palweol)

Lithuanian: Rugpjūtis

Maori: Hereturikōkā

Old English: Wēodmōnaþ

Polish: Sierpień

Russian: август (Avgust)

Sesotho: Phato

Spanish and Portuguese: Agosto

Swahili: Agosti

Thai: Singhakhom

Vietnamese: 胴傪 (tháng tám)

Welsh: Awst

Yiddish: אויגוסט (oygust)

Zulu: uAgasti

August Sayings and Superstitions

Here are some sayings and superstitions associated with the month of August.

General Supersitions

"Agosto, mês do desgosto," or "August, the month of sorrow and grief." (Brazil)

"If a cold August follows a hot July / It foretells a winter hard and dry." (Farming)

If thunderstorms occur in early August, they will continue for the rest of the month.

Don't sail on the second Monday in August, because it was the day the ancient kingdoms of Sodom and Gomorrah were destroyed. (Old seafaring superstition)

If you bathe at midnight on August 1 (Lammas Day) in Lockmaur, Sutherlandshire, you'll be cured of all bodily ailments, but you're expected to repay the Spirit of the Lake with coin. (Scotland)

Wedding Supersitions

"August, better have waited." (Western Kentucky)

"An August bride will be agreeable, And practical as well."

"Married in August's heat and drowse/Lover and friend in your chosen spouse."

"Whoever wed in August be, many a change is sure to see."

The following days in August are considered auspicious for weddings: August 2, 11, 18, 20 and 30.

As for which day of the week to get married, that's easy.

Monday for health, Tuesday for wealth,
Wednesday best of all, Thursday for losses,
Friday for crosses, Saturday for no luck at all.

A Regency wedding proposal

August Symbols

Birthstone: Peridot or sardonyx.

Peridot

Sardonyx (The ancient Cup of the Ptolemies, probably made in
Alexandria, Egypt, in the 1st Century CE)

Birth Flowers: Poppy or Gladiolus, both symbolizing strength of character, love, marriage, and family.

Vase with Cornflowers and Poppies, by Vincent van Gogh

Vase with Red Gladioli, by Vincent van Gogh

"August," by Eugène Grasset

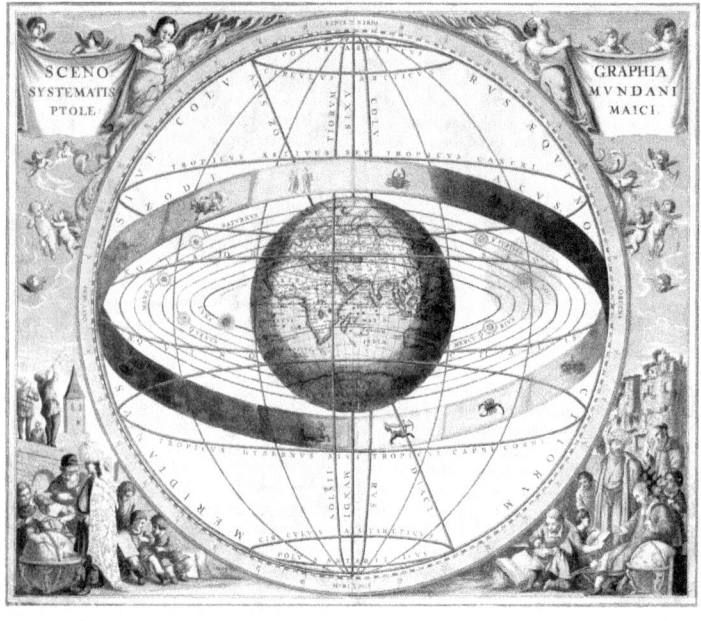

Scenography of the Ptolemaic Cosmography, by Johannes van Loon, based on Andreas Cellarius's *Harmonia Macrocosmica,* 1660

August 8 Zodiac Signs

From the perspective of someone on Earth, the Sun appears to move through the sky throughout the year, along a path astronomers call the *ecliptic plane*. The ecliptic plane is divided into twelve constellations, known as the zodiac, based on traditionally observed patterns of stars. On your birthday, you can't see your constellation, because it's in the daytime sky.

The zodiac was first developed by Babylonian astronomers about 2,500 years ago. Because they were unaware that the Earth wobbles like a spinning top (known as *precession*), they didn't make allowance for the fact that the Sun's path through the zodiac changes over time.

That means there are now two sets of dates for your birth sign. The *tropical dates* are the original Babylonian dates; the *sidereal dates* tell you where the Sun actually appears as it moves along its annual path.

For August 8, the tropical sign is **Leo** and the sidereal sign is **Cancer**.

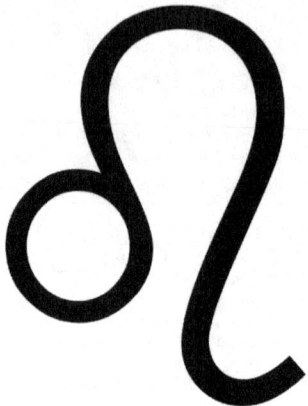

Leo

Tropical July 23 to August 22
Sidereal August 16 to September 15

Leo is one of the earliest recognizable constellations, with its stars forming a sickle or backward question mark. The Mesopotamians, the Persians, the Jews, and the Indians all had a name for the constellation that meant "lion." In Greek mythology, the Nemean lion was impervious to any weapons, but the hero Hercules nevertheless defeated it.

In astrology, Leo is a fire sign, suggesting that Leos are strong-willed and passionate. Leos are supposed to be compatible with Aquarius, Aries, and Sagittarius, but not with Gemini, Capricorn, or Pisces.

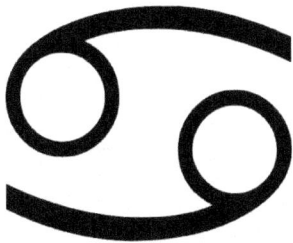

Cancer

Tropical June 21 to July 22
Sidereal July 16 to August 15

The Greek word for "crab" is Καρκινος (Karkinos), later Latinized as carcinus, which evolved into our word cancer. In Greek mythology. In one telling, when Hercules was battling the Hydra, Zeus's wife Hera sent Karkinos to distract the hero, but Hercules kicked it with such force that it was thrown into the sky, becoming a constellation. (Some say that Hercules crushed the crab with his foot and that Hera placed the crab in the night sky as a reward for its service.)

Because of the association with the disease, some astrologers refer to those born under the sign of Cancer as "moon children," because the ruling planet of Cancer is the Moon.

Cancers (or Moon Children) are supposed to be loyal, dependable, caring, and adaptable, but can also be moody, self-pitying, and oversensitive. Cancers are supposed to be particularly compatible with Scorpios, Piceans, and other Cancers.

Illustration by Edward Penfield

What Day of the Week is August 8?

On what day of the week does August 8 fall?

Surprisingly, this isn't an easy question. Because the calendar year is 365 days long (366 in leap years), it doesn't divide evenly by the seven days of the week.

Also, the Earth goes around the Sun in about 365-1/4 days, so a calendar tends to drift over time. That's why the same date falls on different weekdays in different years.

This is made even more complicated by a change in calendars that took place in 1582. Our modern calendar has its roots in ancient Rome, in a calendar reform conducted by Julius Caesar. Caesar commissioned mathematicians to attack the problem, and they came up with the idea of leap years, and thus standardized the calendar for centuries to come. This was called the Julian calendar.

Over time, however, the small errors in Caesar's calculation compounded. That's why Pope Gregory XIII commissioned the Gregorian calendar, used in most of the world today. Some countries converted in 1582, when the calendar was first developed; some converted later; other still haven't changed.

Gregorian and Julian aren't the only types of calendars. The Hebrew year, the Islamic year, and many other calendars are used in different parts of the world and among different people.

You can convert Gregorian dates to other calendars, including the Hebrew calendar, the Islamic calendar, and even the Mayan calendar by visiting the Fourmilab Calendar Converter at http://www.fourmilab.ch/documents/calendar/.

Chinese calendar systems are quite complex and have changed several times; a full discussion is far beyond the scope of this book. If you're interested, you can find information here: http://www.hermetic.ch/cal_stud/chinese_cal.htm.

On Names and Dates

Historians use "CE" (Common Era) and "BCE" (Before the Common Era) instead of the more common "AD" (Anno Domini, or Year of Our Lord) and "BC" (Before Christ), reflecting the fact that the year-numbering system established by the Gregorian calendar is used throughout the world in many countries not culturally Christian.

The CE/BCE designation dates back to at least 1708, and has been adopted as a standard by the United Nations and the Universal Postal Union. Because this series of books covers events and people of all nations and cultures, we use the CE/BCE terms.

The abbreviation "O.S." ("Old Style") on some dates refers to the fact that the Russian Empire did not switch from the Julian to the Gregorian calendar at the same time as the rest of Europe, and therefore some figures and events have two dates.

Also, in the Julian calendar in England in the 16th century, the year began on March 25 rather than January 1. To avoid confusion with Gregorian dates, dates between January and March were often written using both years.

People and events whose original names are not in the Western alphabet have their native names (where possible) in the appropriate script shown in parenthesis. If you are using an e-reader to access an electronic version of this book, all characters don't always display on all devices.

A 50-year brass perpetual calendar.

Quote of the Day

"Time is an illusion, lunchtime doubly so."

Douglas Adams,
from *The Hitchhiker's Guide to the Galaxy*

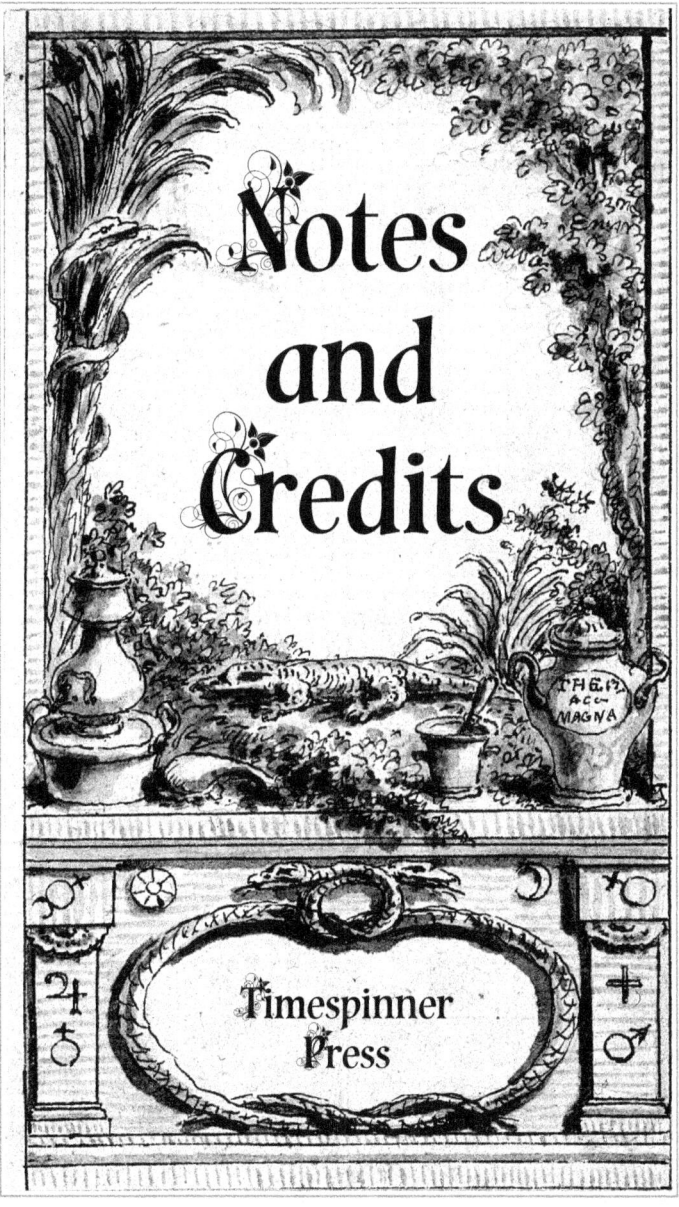

Notes
and
Credits

Timespinner
Press

Cartoon by John T. McCutcheon

Copyright, Credit, and Contact

Follow Us

Our blog "This Day in History" (http://
timespinnerpress.com/this-day-in-history/) features short
articles on events and people associated with each day, and
updates several times each week. Also subscribe to the
"Quote of the Day" at http://timespinnerpress.com/quote-
of-the-day/. You can get daily links by following us on
Facebook at TimespinnerPress, or on Twitter as
@sidewisethinker.

Contact Us

Find an error or a format problem? Want information about
the series, about us, or about when the volume for your
special day might be available? Please email us at
editor@timespinnerpress.com. (We also take requests if your
special day isn't yet complete. Please give us at least six
weeks' notice if possible.)

Sources

We owe a great debt to Wikipedia, which is our first stop for
research. We attempt to make independent confirmation of
all important dates and facts through a variety of other
sources.

Other sources we frequently use include the Library of
Congress; "on this day" listings from *Encyclopedia Britannica*,
the *New York Times*, and the BBC; Omniglot for the names of
months in other languages; *Chase's Calendar of Events;* and, of
course, the always essential Google.

All art and photographs are either in the public domain, used under a Creative Commons license, or with a "fair use" justification, and most frequently come from Wikimedia Commons and the Library of Congress Prints and Photographs Division.

Attribution is provided where possible, or as requested by the copyright owner, or when there is particular historical significance, listed below. For information about any particular illustration or photograph, please contact us.

Credits

1. The cover painting "Defeat of the Spanish Armada 8 August 1588" was painted by Philip James de Loutherbourg in 1796, and is in the public domain because its copyright has expired. The original can be found in the collection of the National Maritime Museum, Greenwich Hospital Collection, London.

2. The illustration of the month of July used on the back cover is from the French Gothic illuminated manuscript *Les Très Riches Heures du duc de Berry* by the Limbourg Brothers, Jean Colombe, and an intermediate painter whose name is lost to history. It is in the public domain because its copyright has expired.

3. The box graphic used on the first page is from a 1916 pamphlet entitled "Divorce versus Democracy" authored by G. K. Chesterton, originally published in London by the Society of St. Peter and St. Paul. It is in the public domain in the US because it was published prior to 1923, and is in the public domain in all countries (including the country of origin) in which the copyright time is the author's life plus 70 years or less.

4. The graphic design for the section pages in this book is from a design originally created for a pharmacy label. It is courtesy of Wellcome Images (ICV No 11073, photo V0010813), and is used here under CC BY-SA 4.0.

5.   The painting *The Spanish Armada Leaving the Port of Ferrol* by Sir Oswald W. Brierly is from the 19th century, and is in the public domain because its copyright has expired. The original can be found in the National Maritime Museum, London. The image has been cropped.

6.   The map of the route of the Spanish Armada was created by cartographer Frank Martini, History Department, United States Military Academy, West Point, New York. It is in the public domain as a work created by an employee or officer of the US Army.

7.   The 1892 painting *Destrucción de la Armada Invencible* by José Gartner de la Peña is in the public domain because its copyright has expired. It can be found in the Museo de Arte Moderno.

8.   The photograph of a Wright Model A at Le Mans, France, is courtesy of the US Air Force Historical Research Agency, and is in the public domain as a work of a US military member or employee as part of that person's official duties.

9.   The 1889 advertisement for the Edison Mimeograph is in the public domain because its copyright has expired.

10. The photograph of the first flight of the XB-36 is courtesy of the US Air Force, and is in the public domain as a work of a US military member or employee as part of that person's official duties.

11. The cover photograph from the album *Abbey Road* is not in the public domain, and is used here under "fair use" provisions of the US copyright code. The use of the image is to illustrate a historically significant event, no free alternatives exist, and the images is printed in too low a resolution to be suitable in pirate or other unauthorized uses.

12. The 1864 painting *Submarine Torpedo Boat H. L. Hunley, December 6, 1863*, by Conrad Wise Chapman, is in the public domain because its copyright has expired. The original can be found in the American Civil War Museum, Richmond, Virginia.

13. The publicity photograph of Fay Wray is in the public domain because it was first published in the United States between1923 and 1977 without a copyright notice.

Traditionally, publicity photographs are not copyrighted because of the way in which they are intended to be used.

14. The 1910 photograph of Matthew Henson is from the Library of Congress Prints and Photographs Division (LC-USZC4-7503). It is in the public domain because its copyright has expired.

15. The photograph of Emiliano Zapata is from the George Grantham Bain collection at the Library of Congress. According to the library, there are no known copyright restrictions on the use of this work.

16. The 1919 photograph of Sara Teasdale was taken by Arnold Genthe.It is in the public domain because its copyright has expired.

17. The 1946 photograph of Benny Carter is from the William P. Gottlieb collection at the Library of Congress. In accordance with the wishes of William Gottlieb, the photographs in this collection entered into the public domain on February 16, 2010.

18. The 1968 publicity photograph of Dustin Hoffman from the Broadway play *Jimmy Shine* is in the public domain because it was first published in the United States between1923 and 1977 without a copyright notice. Traditionally, publicity photographs are not copyrighted because of the way in which they are intended to be used.

19. The 1950 publicity photograph of Esther Williams is in the public domain because it was first published in the United States between1923 and 1977 without a copyright notice. Traditionally, publicity photographs are not copyrighted because of the way in which they are intended to be used.

20. The 1934 photograph of Stanley Livingston and Ernest O. Lawrence in front of the 27-in cyclotron at the University of California Berkeley is from the US National Archives (ARCH 558593). It is in the public domain as a work created by an employee of the US government as part of that person's official duties.

21. The 1971 photograph of Jerry Tarkanian surrounded by his players is in the public domain as a work created by an employee of the State of California as part of that person's official duties.

22. The 1952 publicity photograph of Patricia Neal is in the public domain because it was first published in the United States between1923 and 1977 without a copyright notice. Traditionally, publicity photographs are not copyrighted because of the way in which they are intended to be used.

23. The circa 1929 photograph of Louise Brooks is from the George Grantham Bain collection at the Library of Congress. According to the library, there are no known copyright restrictions on the use of this work.

24. The publicity photograph of the cast of *The Dick Van Dyke Show* is in the public domain because it was first published in the United States between1923 and 1977 without a copyright notice. Traditionally, publicity photographs are not copyrighted because of the way in which they are intended to be used.

25. The scorebook from the 1916 World Series is in the public domain because its copyright has expired.

26. The 1895 painting "Young Ballerina Holding a Black Cat" is by Pierre Carrier-Belleuse, and is in the public domain because its copyright has expired.

27. The 2009 photograph of the sign for Andy's Frozen Custard was taken by Jose Kevo, and is used here under CC BY-SA 2.0.

28. The 1815 woodcut of a proposal is in the public domain because its copyright has expired.

29. The 1943 photograph of a Buffalo, New York, nursery school for children of working mothers was taken by Marjory Collins for the Office of War Information. It is in the public domain as a work created by an employee of the US federal government. The original photo is in the collection of the Library of Congress, digital ID fsa.8d18633.

30. The painting "August" is from the *Brevarium Grimani,* circa 1510, and is in the public domain because its copyright has expired.

31. The 1815 woodcut of a proposal is in the public domain because its copyright has expired.

32. The photograph of an emerald cut peridot was taken by Michelle Jo, who released it into the public domain in 2009.

33. The photograph of the Cup of the Ptolemies was taken by "Clio20" and is used here under CC BY-SA 3.0. The cup is in the collection of the Bibliothèque Nationale de France.

34. The 1886 paintings *Vase with Cornflowers and Poppies* by Vincent van Gogh are in the public domain because its copyright has expired.

35. The 1886 paintings *Vase with Red Gladioli* and Vase with Cornflowers and Poppies by Vincent van Gogh are in the public domain because its copyright has expired.

36. The 1896 illustration "August" by Eugène Grasset is in the public domain because its copyright has expired.

37. The celestial sphere is from *Scenography of the Ptolemaic Cosmography*, by Johannes van Loon, based on Andreas Cellarius's *Harmonia Macrocosmica*, 1660. It is in the public domain because its copyright has expired.

38. The 1906 automobile calendar is by Edward Penfield, and is in the collection of the Library of Congress Prints and Photographs Division. It is in the public domain because its copyright has expired.

39. The 50-year perpetual calendar photograph is in the public domain.

40. The cartoon by John T. McCutcheon is from his 1905 collection *The Mysterious Stranger and Other Cartoons* by John T. McCutcheon. It is in the public domain because its copyright has expired.

License Description and Terms

Aside from material purely in the public domain, photographs and other material in this book are used under specific licenses permitting free use, usually with an attribution requirement. For full text and terms of these licenses, click or enter the appropriate links below. If you believe there is an error in the copyright status or attribution of any of these images, please email us.

- Creative Commons Attribution 2.0 Generic (CC-BY 2.0): http://creativecommons.org/licenses/by/2.0/deed.en
- Creative Commons Attribution-Share Alike 3.0 Generic (CC-BY-SA 3.0): http://creativecommons.org/licenses/by-sa/3.0/
- Creative Commons Attribution-Share Alike 2.5 Generic (CC-BY-SA 2.5): http://creativecommons.org/licenses/by-sa/2.5/deed.en
- Creative Commons Attribution-Share Alike 2.0 Generic (CC-BY-SA 2.0): http://creativecommons.org/licenses/by/2.0/deed.en
- Creative Commons Attribution-Share Alike 1.0 Generic (CC-BY-SA 1.0): http://creativecommons.org/licenses/by-sa/1.0/deed.en
- CC0 1.0 Universal (CC0 1.0) Public Domain Dedication (CC0 1.0) http://creativecommons.org/publicdomain/zero/1.0/deed.en
- GNU Free Documentation License (GFDL): http://en.wikipedia.org/wiki/Wikipedia:Text_of_the_GNU_Free_Documentation_License
- License Art Libre (Free Art License): http://artlibre.org

Timespinner
Press

Other Books from Timespinner Press

The Story of a Special Day
Michael Dobson

A series of (eventually) 366 volumes covering everything that happened on your special day! Events, births, deaths, quotes, holidays, and much more. It's like a birthday card they'll never throw away!

US$7.95 print / US$2.99 ebook.

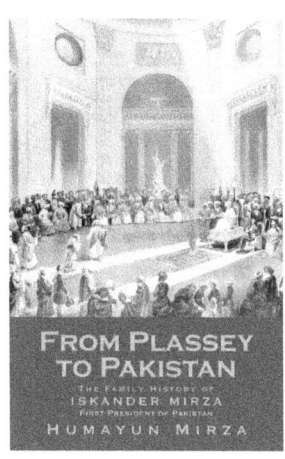

From Plassey to Pakistan
Humayun Mirza

The history of British Colonial India and the formation of Pakistan from the unique perspective of the son of Pakistan's first president and last of the royal line of Bengal, Bihar, and Orissa! This unique historical document tells the inside story of this distinguished family, including the detailed story of the coup that toppled his father from power!

US$27.95 print

A Whole New Navy: America's War in the Pacific

Miles Durr

The most comprehensive and detailed description of America's naval war in the Pacific ever—every battle, every ship, every task force and every task group from Pearl Harbor through the Japanese surrender! A must-have for the collection of every World War II buff!

US$29.95 print

Improbable History: The Weird, the Obscure, and the Strangely Important

edited by Michael Dobson

From the birth of Western civilization to the rescue of Apollo 13, from the Leaning Tower of Pisa to Florence's Duomo, history has often turned on small, improbable details. Whatever happened to the ancient Samaritan people? Why did a fortuitous rainstorm allow the British to conquer India? How did an air raid in Italy lead to the development of chemotherapy? What happened when Albert Einstein met Adolf Hitler on the streets of Berlin? How did the Japanese manage to attack the US mainland using balloons? A cast of award-winning writers tackle some of the strangest tales in history!

US$19.95 print